MW00564555

Stay with Me, Sing & More Hot Singles

ISBN 978-1-4950-0215-1

HAL•LEONARD®
CORPORATION

7777 W. BLUEMOUND RD. P.O. BOX 13819 MILWAUKEE, WI 53213

Visit Hal Leonard Online at
www.halleonard.com

AM I WRONG

Words and Music by VINCENT DERY,
NICOLAY SEREBA, WILLIAM WIIK LARSEN
and ABDOULIE JALLOW

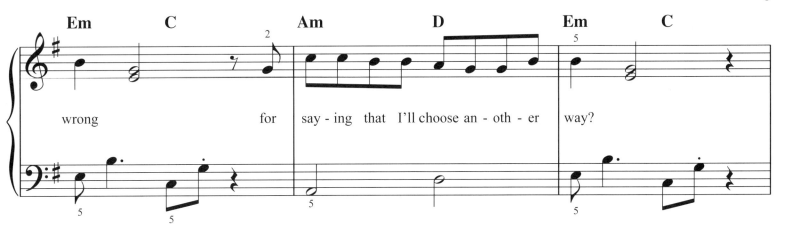

wrong for say - ing that I'll choose an - oth - er way?

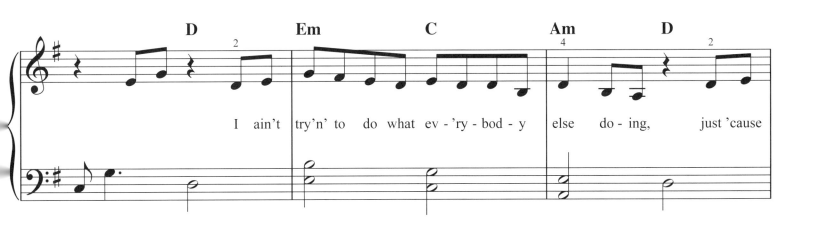

I ain't try'n' to do what ev - 'ry - bod - y else do - ing, just 'cause

ev - 'ry - bod - y do - ing what they all do. If one thing I know, I'll

fall but I'll grow. I'm walk-ing down _ this road of mine, _ this road that I _____ call home. So am I

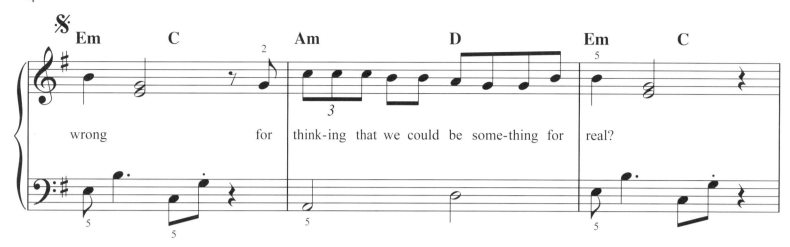

wrong   for   think-ing that we could be some-thing for   real?

Now, am I   wrong   for   try-ing to reach the things that   I   can't

see?   That's just how I   feel.   (Ooh.) _____

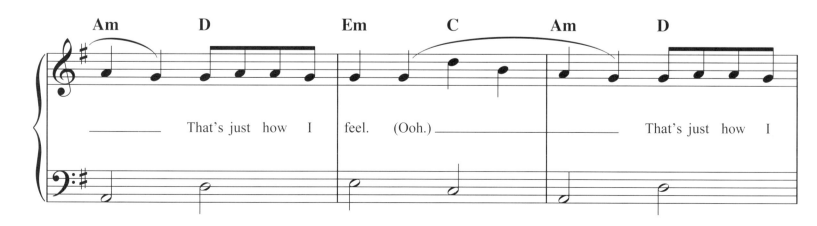

_____ That's just how I   feel.   (Ooh.) _____   That's just how I

To Coda

feel._____   Try - ing to reach the things that   I   can't   see.   (Ooh.)_____

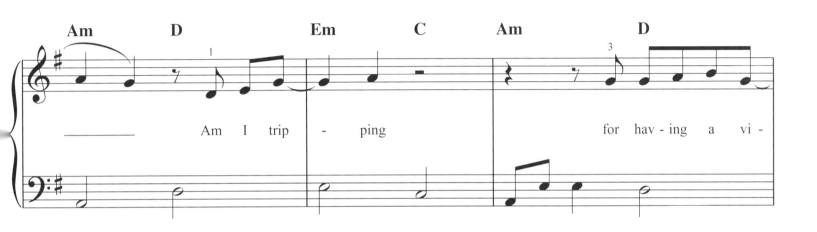

_____ Am I trip - ping   for hav - ing a vi -

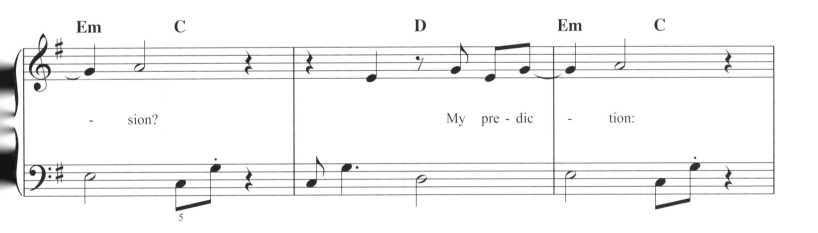

- sion?   My pre - dic - tion:

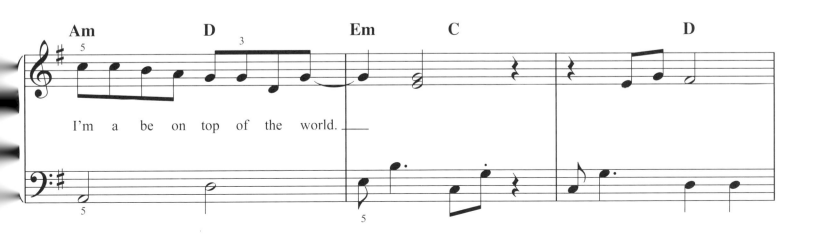

I'm a be on top of the world.____

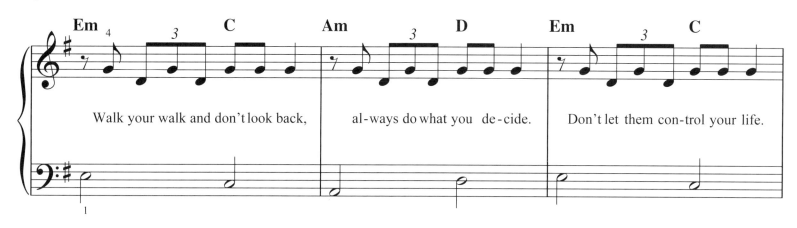

Walk your walk and don't look back, al-ways do what you de-cide. Don't let them con-trol your life.

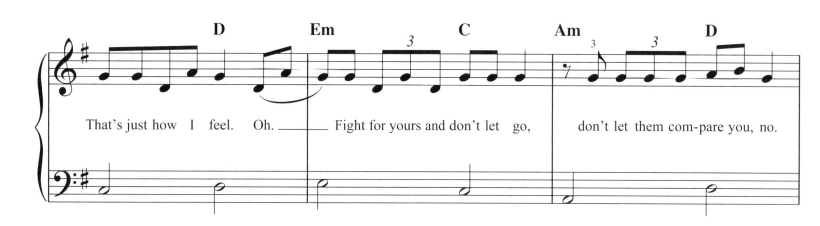

That's just how I feel. Oh.____ Fight for yours and don't let go, don't let them com-pare you, no.

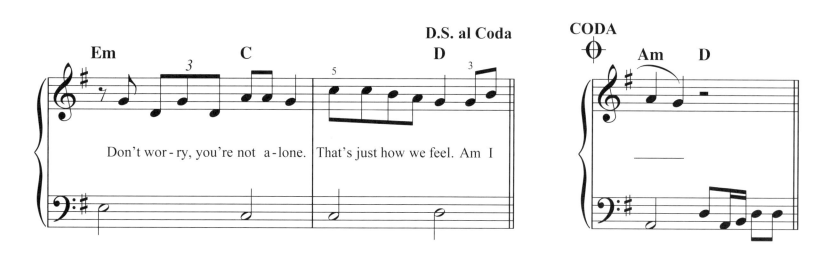

Don't wor-ry, you're not a-lone. That's just how we feel. Am I

Don't wor-ry, you're not a-lone. That's just how we feel. Am I

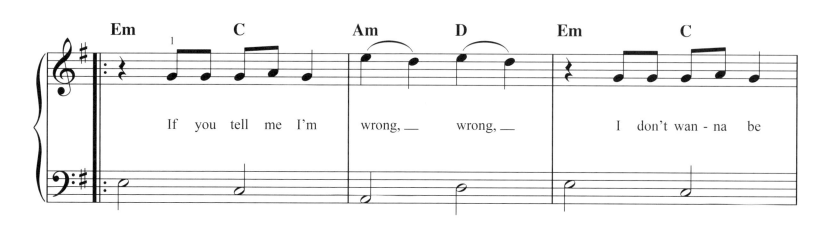

If you tell me I'm wrong,___ wrong,___ I don't wan-na be

right, _____ right. _____ If you tell me I'm wrong, _____ wrong, _____

I don't wan - na be right. _____ Am I

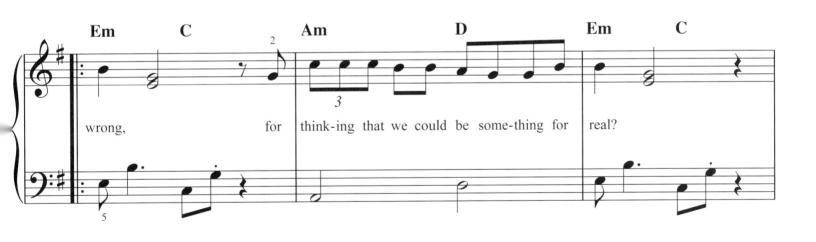

wrong, for think-ing that we could be some-thing for real?

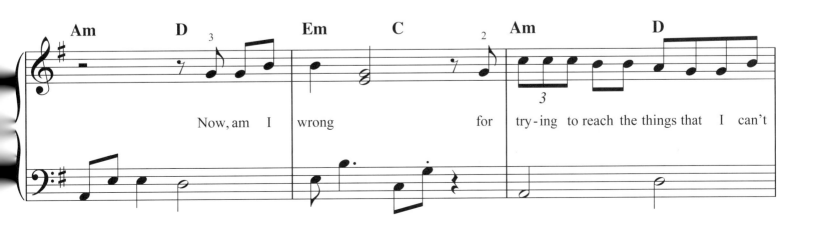

Now, am I wrong for try-ing to reach the things that I can't

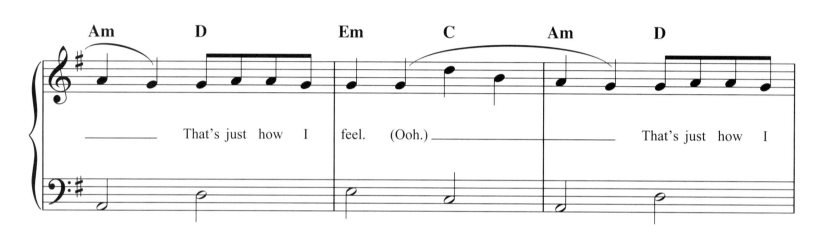

BOOM CLAP
from the Motion Picture Soundtrack THE FAULT IN OUR STARS

Words and Music by CHARLOTTE AITCHISON,
PATRIK BERGER, FREDRIK BERGER
and STEFAN GRASLUND

Moderate Pop Rock

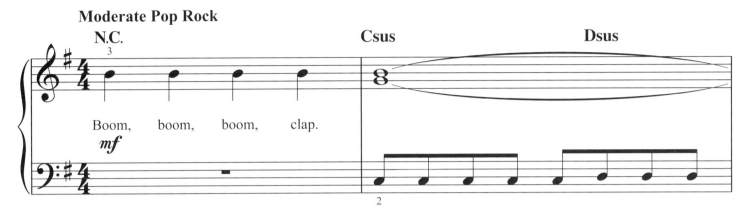

Boom, boom, boom, clap.

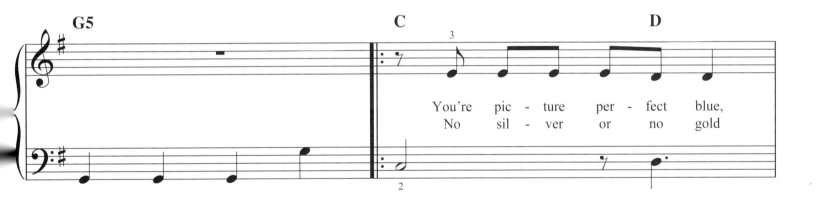

You're pic - ture per - fect blue,
No sil - ver or no gold

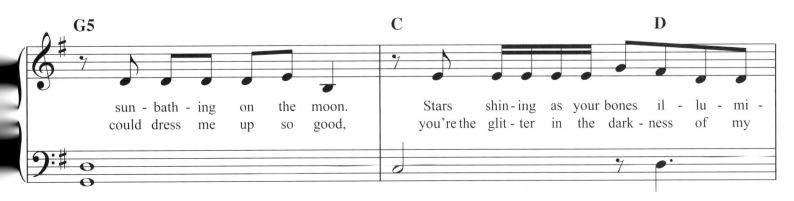

sun - bath - ing on the moon.
could dress me up so good,

Stars shin - ing as your bones il - lu - mi -
you're the glit - ter in the dark - ness of my

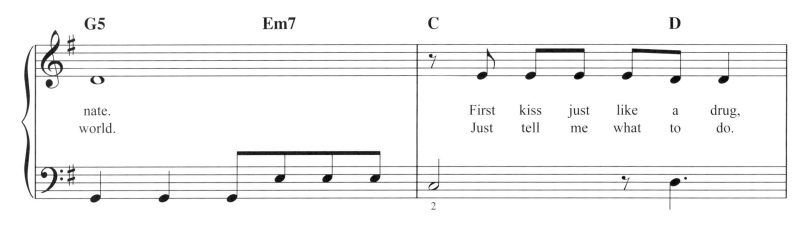

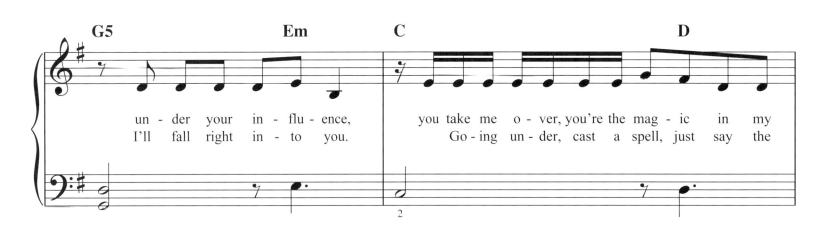

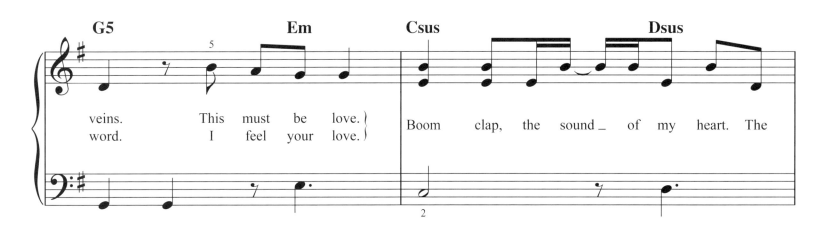

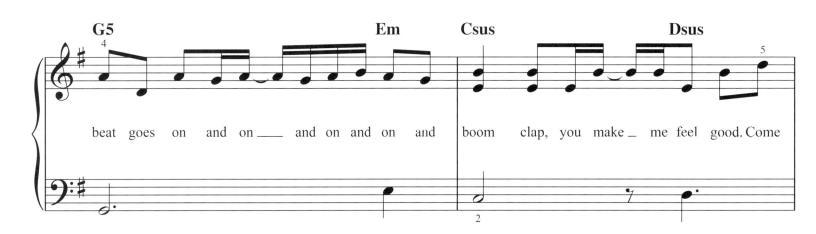

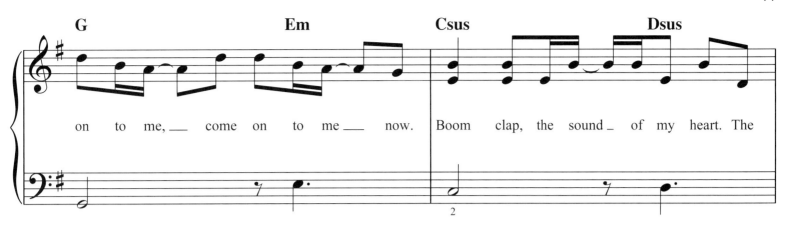

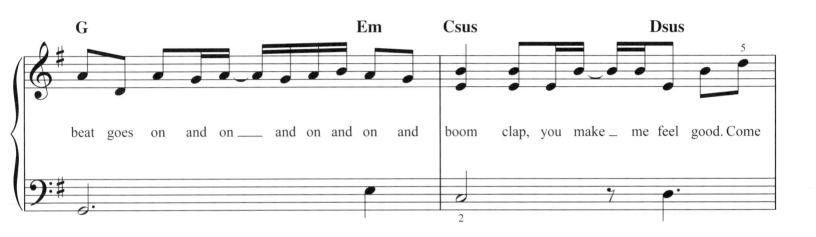

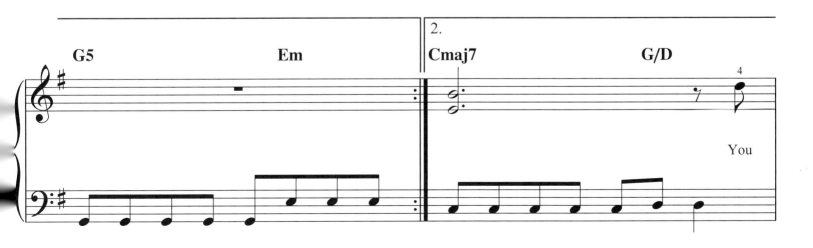

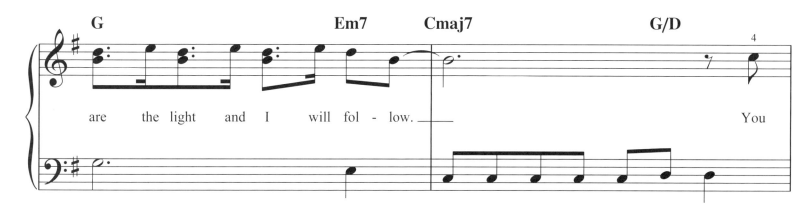

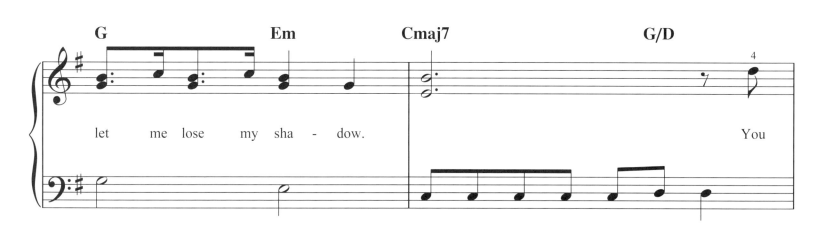

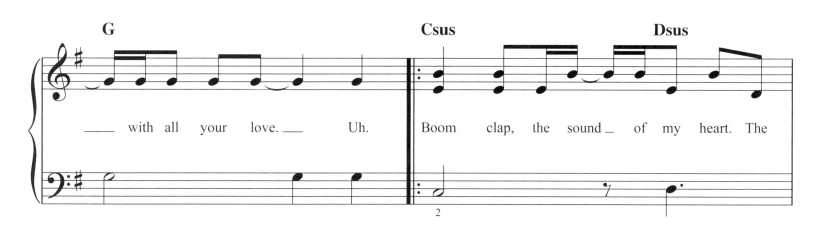

LOVE RUNS OUT

Words and Music by RYAN TEDDER,
BRENT KUTZLE, ZACHARY FILKINS,
EDDIE FISHER and ANDREW BROWN

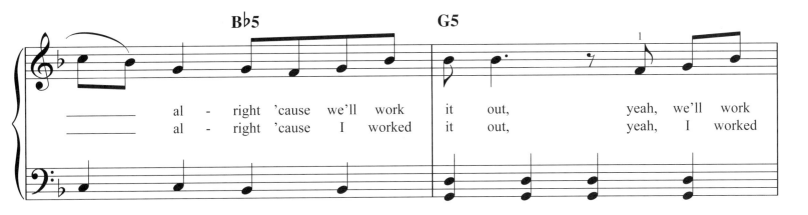

al - right 'cause we'll work it out, yeah, we'll work
al - right 'cause I worked it out, yeah, I worked

it out.
it out. I'll be do - in' this, if you have a doubt, 'til the love

runs out, 'til the love runs out. I'll be your

1. runs out. I got my

mind made up. Man, I can't let go. ___ I'm kill - in' ev - 'ry sec - ond 'til it

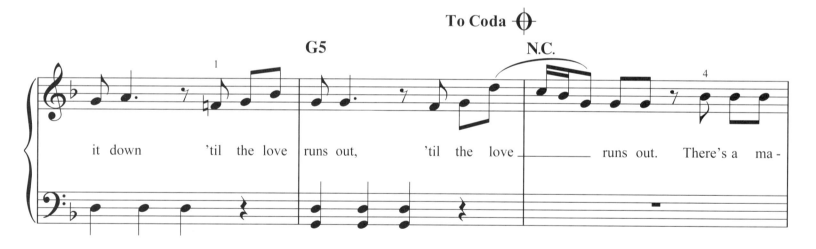

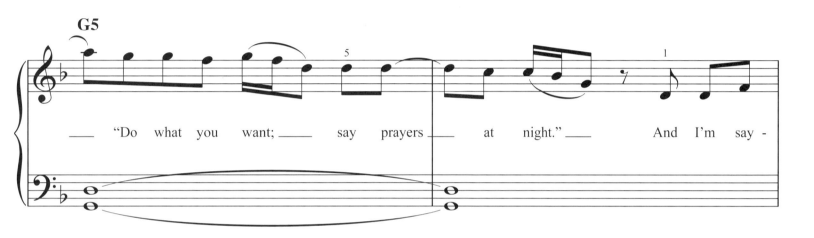

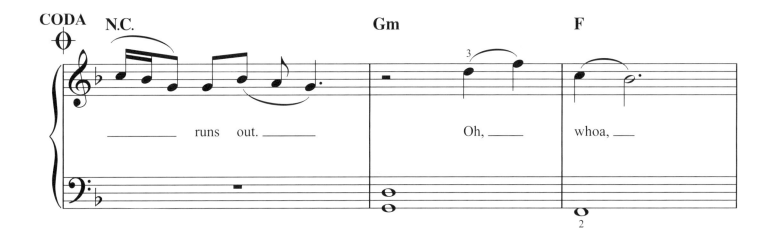

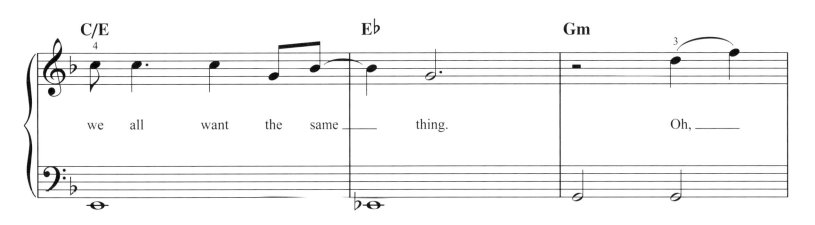

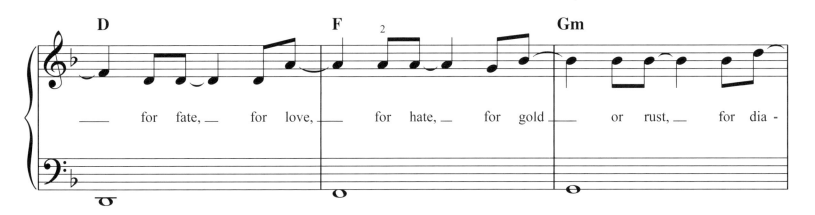

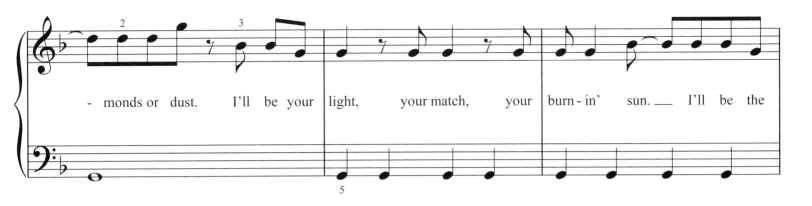

- monds or dust. I'll be your light, your match, your burn-in' sun. ___ I'll be the

bright in black that's mak-in' you run. ___ I've got my

mind made up. Man, I can't let go. ___ I'm kill-in' ev-'ry sec-ond 'til it

saves my soul. ___ Ooh, _____ I'll be run-nin', ooh, _____

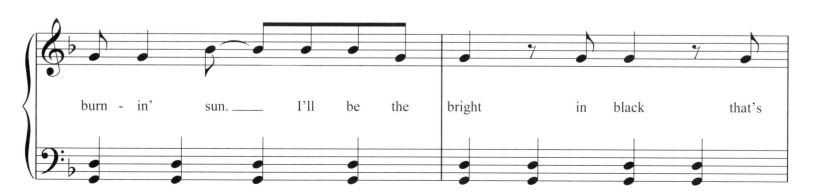

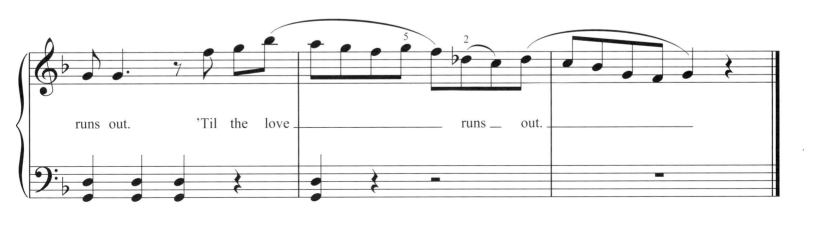

STAY WITH ME

Words and Music by SAM SMITH,
JAMES NAPIER and WILLIAM EDWARD PHILLIPS

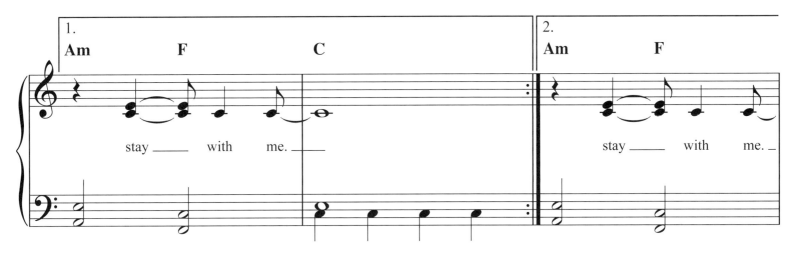

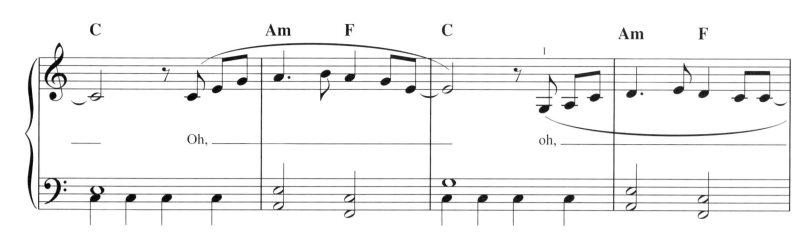

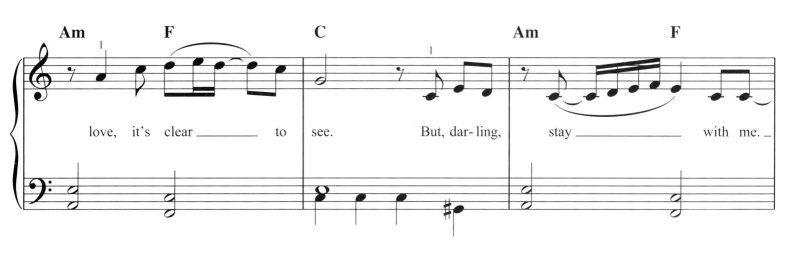

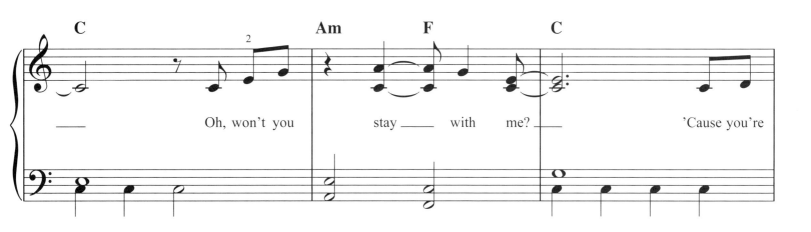

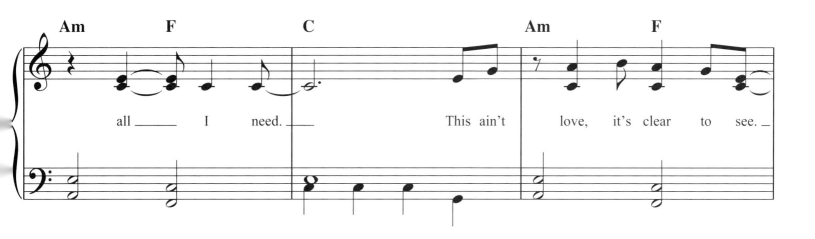

SING

Words and Music by ED SHEERAN
and PHARRELL WILLIAMS

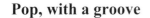

Pop, with a groove

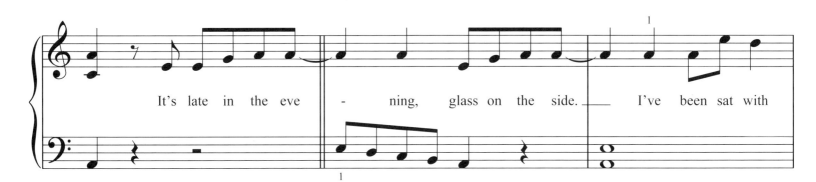

It's late in the eve - ning, glass on the side. I've been sat with

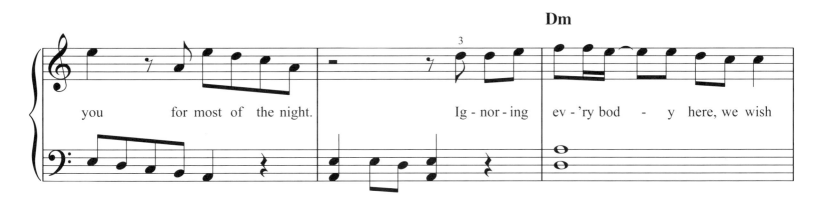

you for most of the night. Ig - nor - ing ev - 'ry bod - y here, we wish

they would dis - ap-pear. So may-be we could get down now.

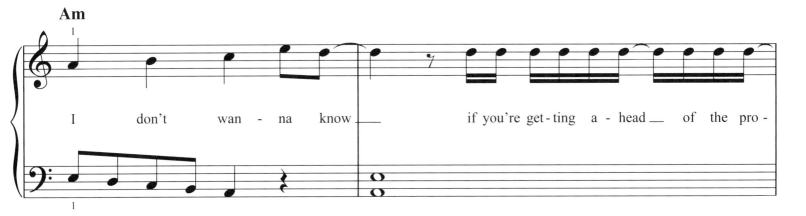

Am

I don't wan - na know___ if you're get - ting a - head___ of the pro -

- gram. I want you to ___ be mine, la - dy, _____ and to

Dm

hold your bod - y close.___ Take an - oth - er step in - to the no -

- man's land for the long - est time, la - dy. _____ I

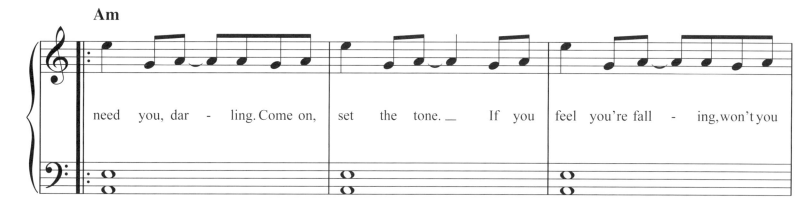

need you, dar - ling. Come on, set the tone. __ If you feel you're fall - ing, won't you

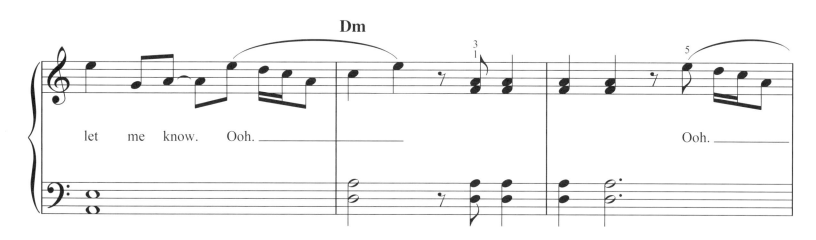

let me know. Ooh. ___ Ooh. ___

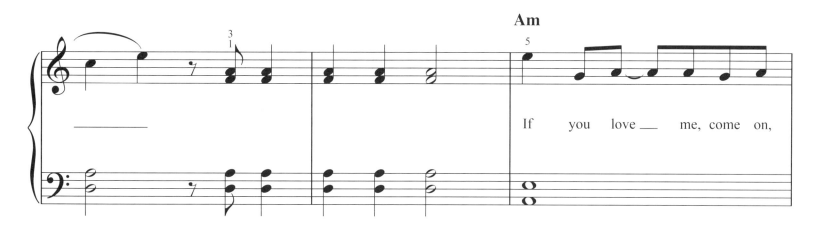

___ If you love __ me, come on,

get in - volved. __ Feel it rush - ing through __ you from your head to toe. __ Ooh. ___

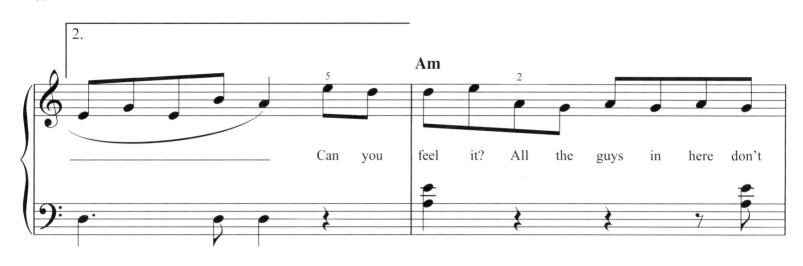

Can you feel it? All the guys in here don't

e - ven wan - na dance. _ Can you feel _ it? All that I can hear is

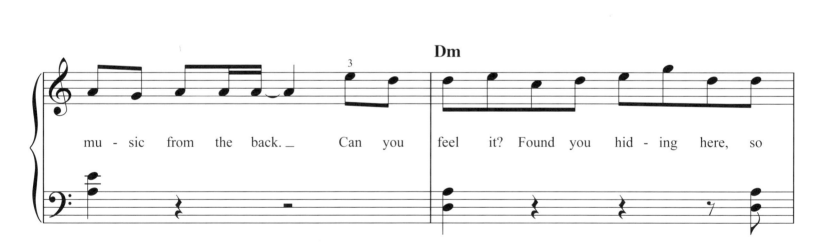

mu - sic from the back. _ Can you feel it? Found you hid - ing here, so

won't you take my hand, _ dar - ling, be - fore the beat kicks in a -

need   you, dar - ling. Come on,   set   the   tone. ___   If   you
If   you love ___ me, come on,   get   in - volved. _   Feel   it

feel   you're fall - ing, won't you   let   me   know. __ }
rush - ing through _ you from your   head   to   toe. ___ }   Ooh. _____

_____   Ooh. _____

_____   Sing!